The Night Before Christmas

CLEMENT MOORE

Illustrated by Tomie dePaola

OXFORD
UNIVERSITY PRESS

OXFORD
UNIVERSITY PRESS

Great Clarendon Street, Oxford OX2 6DP

Oxford University Press is a department of the University of Oxford.
It furthers the University's objective of excellence in research, scholarship,
and education by publishing worldwide in

Oxford New York

Auckland Bangkok Buenos Aires Cape Town
Chennai Dar es Salaam Delhi Istanbul Karachi
Kolkata Kuala Lumpur Madrid Melbourne Mexico City Mumbai
Nairobi São Paulo Shanghai Taipei Tokyo Toronto

Oxford is a registered trade mark of Oxford University Press
in the UK and in certain other countries

Illustrations copyright © Tomie dePaola 1980

The moral rights of the artist have been asserted

Database right Oxford University Press (maker)

First published 1980 by Holiday House, New York
First published in this edition 2004

British Library Cataloguing in Publication Data available

ISBN 0 19 279182 6

1 3 5 7 9 10 8 6 4 2

Printed in Malaysia

FOR ALL MY NEIGHBORS

W. F. '80   T. deP.

'TWAS
the night before Christmas,
when all through the house
Not a creature was stirring,
not even a mouse;

The stockings were hung
by the chimney with care,
In hopes that St. Nicholas
soon would be there;

The children were nestled
all snug in their beds,
While visions of sugarplums
danced in their heads;

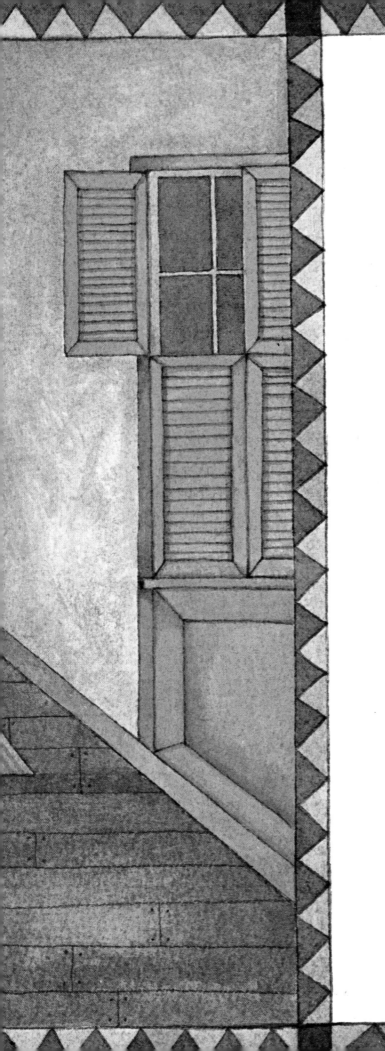

And Mamma in her 'kerchief,
and I in my cap,
Had just settled our brains
for a long winter's nap;

When out on the lawn
        there arose such a clatter,
I sprang from the bed
        to see what was the matter.
Away to the window
        I flew like a flash,
Tore open the shutters
        and threw up the sash.

The moon on the breast
   of the new-fallen snow,
Gave the lustre of midday
   to objects below,
When, what to my wondering
   eyes should appear,

But a miniature sleigh,
    and eight tiny reindeer,
With a little old driver,
    so lively and quick,
I knew in a moment
    it must be St. Nick.

More rapid than eagles
        his coursers they came,
And he whistled, and shouted,
        and called them by name;
"Now, *Dasher*! Now, *Dancer*!
        Now, *Prancer* and *Vixen*!
On, *Comet*! On, *Cupid*!
        On, *Donder* and *Blitzen*!
To the top of the porch!
        To the top of the wall!
Now dash away! Dash away!
        Dash away all!"

As dry leaves that before
the wild hurricane fly,
When they meet with an obstacle,
mount to the sky;
So up to the housetop
the coursers they flew,

With the sleigh full of toys,
   and St. Nicholas too.
And then in a twinkling,
   I heard on the roof,
The prancing and pawing
   of each little hoof—

As I drew in my head,
    and was turning around,
Down the chimney St. Nicholas
    came with a bound.

He was dressed all in fur,
　　　from his head to his foot,
And his clothes were all tarnished
　　　with ashes and soot;
A bundle of toys
　　　he had flung on his back,
And he looked like a pedlar
　　　just opening his pack.

His eyes—how they twinkled!
    His dimples, how merry!
His cheeks were like roses,
    his nose like a cherry!
His droll little mouth
    was drawn up like a bow,
And the beard of his chin
    was as white as the snow;

The stump of his pipe
    he held tight in his teeth,
And the smoke it encircled
    his head like a wreath;
He had a broad face
    and a little round belly,
That shook when he laughed,
    like a bowlful of jelly.

He was chubby and plump,
    a right jolly old elf,
And I laughed when I saw him,
    in spite of myself,
A wink of his eye
    and a twist of his head,
Soon gave me to know
    I had nothing to dread;

He spoke not a word,
    but went straight to his work,
And filled all the stockings;
    then turned with a jerk,
And laying his finger
    aside of his nose,
And giving a nod,
    up the chimney he rose;

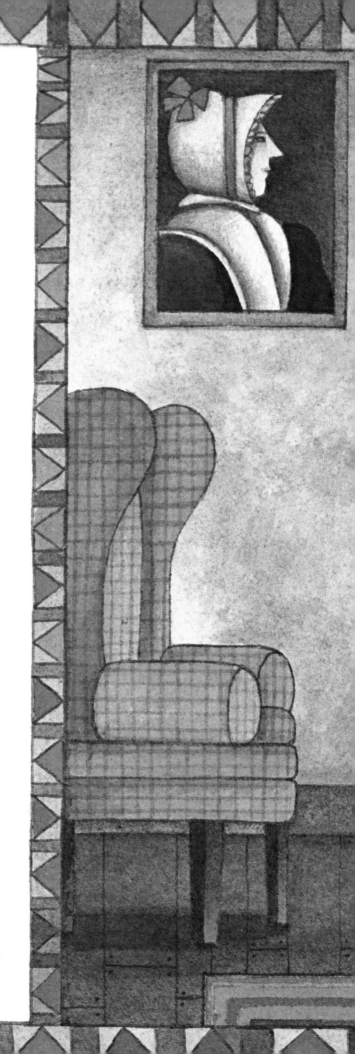

He sprang to his sleigh,
  to his team gave a whistle,
And away they all flew
  like the down of a thistle.

But I heard him exclaim,
    ere he drove out of sight,
"Happy Christmas to all.
    And to all a good night."

About This Edition

Clement Moore, who was a professor at General Theological Seminary, wrote *The Night Before Christmas* for his children in 1822. The poem was originally called *A Visit from St. Nicholas* and was first published in the newspaper, *Troy Sentinel*, in 1823.

Tomie de Paola has set the poem in the 1840's, using his own home in a small New Hampshire village as a model. His borders are based on designs from New England quilts, many of which he owns.